W9-BKD-702

FALCON FLIGHT

ALSO BY ADA AND FRANK GRAHAM

Whale Watch (1)
Bug Hunters (2)
Coyote Song (4)

AN AUDUBON READER

FALCON FLIGHT

ADA AND FRANK GRAHAM
ILLUSTRATIONS BY D. D. TYLER

DELACORTE PRESS/NEW YORK

Published by
Delacorte Press
1 Dag Hammarskjold Plaza
New York, New York 10017

Library of Congress Cataloging in Publication Data

Graham, Ada.
    Falcon flight.

    (An Audubon reader)
    Includes index.
    SUMMARY: Describes recent efforts to save the vanishing
peregrine falcon, a frequent object of indiscriminate
hunting due to misconceptions surrounding birds of prey.
    1. Peregrine falcon—Juvenile literature. 2. Birds
of prey—Juvenile literature. 3. Birds, Protection of—
Juvenile literature. [1. Peregrine falcon. 2. Falcons.
3. Birds of prey. 4. Wildlife conservation]
I. Graham, Frank, 1925–   joint author. II. Tyler,
D. D. III. Title. IV. Series.
QL696.F34G73   639'.97'891   78-50442
ISBN 0-440-02485-4
ISBN 0-440-02486-2 lib. bdg.

To the memory of Marie Rodell,
conservationist and helpful friend
to so many of us who write about the natural world,
this book is dedicated.

CONTENTS

1

THE TOWER

One morning at the beginning of June 1975, a small crowd of men and women gathered at the foot of a tall tower on Carroll Island near Aberdeen, Maryland. The island was a part of the U.S. Army's Aberdeen Proving Grounds, where weapons are tested. Only a few years before, shells containing poison gas were test-fired from the tower. On this day, however, the tower was to be the site of a very different kind of experiment.

A biologist carefully climbed an iron ladder to the top of the tower, seventy-five feet above the ground. He carried a large cardboard box that held four nervous, screeching young peregrine falcons. When he reached the

Peregrine falcons, "the world's most successful birds."

top, the biologist put the birds into a larger plywood box fixed to the tower.

The birds had been hatched in captivity at Cornell University and brought to Aberdeen in a station wagon. Now they were going into a new and temporary home. This transfer was part of a daring and imaginative plan to bring back one of the world's most magnificent birds to a vast region of the northeastern United States.

The peregrine had somehow managed to survive shooting, trapping, nest robbing, and the disturbance of its breeding places by the spread of civilization. But it could not survive the poisons people poured into the environment.

Now, in the 1970s, men and women all over the country began to work together to bring back the peregrine. At Carroll Island that day the crowd had been welcomed by an officer of the U.S. Army, which was helping to make the program a success by putting the tower aside for the birds' use. Government officials, university biologists, conservationists, and members of the press were among the people on the island.

The biologist left the peregrine chicks in the big plywood box on the tower and descended to the ground. The birds were thirty-two days old and hardly looked like the fierce falcons they would grow up to be. In fact, as one student of birds has said, at that age the peregrines "look like young chickens wrapped in white fox fur." Fluffy white down covered their bodies. Here and there the dark tips of real feathers showed through the fluff.

The young peregrines were in the right place. Their box was high and isolated. When peregrine falcons still nested in the wild in the eastern United States, they usually chose ledges on steep cliffs on which to raise their young.

The box provided plenty of room for the chicks. It was about three feet high. In one of the sides there was an opening covered with metal bars. Perched on small rocks in their box, the young peregrines were able to look out over the island and its trees.

Carroll Island was a good location for the peregrine experiment. It was army property, protected from people who might want to bother the young birds. There were no foxes or owls that might kill the peregrines when they were first released on the island and still unable to defend themselves properly. And in the marshes there were flocks of small birds that these hunting falcons could capture and eat.

For several weeks, however, the biologists would have to take care of the peregrines. They were not yet able to fly or hunt. When it was time to feed them a biologist climbed the ladder, opened a wooden door in the bottom of the box, and slid in meals of chopped quail or pigeon.

Falcon Flight

The little falcons did not see their human helpers—they were already learning to be wild.

There was only one bad moment. A few days after the peregrines had been put in their new home, a fierce storm struck the island. Thunder boomed and lightning flashed across the sky. One of the biologists, afraid for the birds' lives, rushed up the ladder and removed them to safety. Within minutes lightning hit the tower, badly damaging their home.

Soon the box was repaired, this time with lightning rods attached to it. The peregrines went back to the tower. They grew rapidly, their bodies darkening as the feathers poked out through the down and covered their faces, wings, and tails.

The chicks were becoming restless. They looked curiously out through the bars at the small birds that flew across the island. Often during the day they flapped their long, pointed wings, exercising the flight muscles that make adult peregrines among the strongest flyers in the world.

The time was coming when they would need strength and skill, flying free.

PREY

prey. It captures and
~~cats other~~ ~~~~ ~~~~ of this characteristic,
the birds of prey have aroused either admiration or
hatred among people all over the world.

Of course the statement that any animal kills—or
preys on—other living things doesn't tell very much
about it. Animals may be divided between the predators
and the creatures they prey upon. Man himself evolved
as a predator. The lion that feeds on an antelope, the cat
that feeds on a mouse, and the ladybird beetle that feeds
on aphids are predators. In a sense, the chickadee that
eats a caterpillar, the robin that eats a worm, and the
pelican that eats a fish are also birds of prey.

But, for convenience, scientists describe only certain
orders of birds as "birds of prey." One of these orders is

5

made up of the owls, which hunt mostly by night. The other order is the Falconiformes, birds that have hooked bills and strong feet armed with claws or talons.

Falconiformes fly by daylight and eat the flesh of other living things such as mammals, birds, fish, snakes, frogs, and insects. We usually refer to them as hawks or hawklike birds. Among them are the vultures, the eagles, the kites, the true hawks, and the falcons.

This group of birds has fascinated human beings because they vary so much in their shapes and habits. They range in size from the condors—huge American vultures—whose wings measure ten feet or more from tip to tip, down to the falconets, which are the size of a sparrow and weigh only one tenth of a pound. Their hunting habits also vary greatly. The golden eagle soars high in the sky scanning the countryside far below for its prey. The secretary bird stalks on its long legs across the African plains, looking for snakes, which it kills by striking them with its powerful foot and then battering them with its flailing wings.

Human beings—even those who don't care much about birds one way or the other—have always noticed the birds of prey and classified them as good or bad, brave or cowardly, noble or cruel. Hardly anyone ever has a good word to say about vultures. Yet they are among the most beneficial of all birds because they clean up dead animals that otherwise might remain in the environment and breed disease.

"People just don't give much thought to their feelings about vultures," says John Borneman, a biologist who studies condors for the National Audubon Society. "Sometimes a man will come up to me and say that he can't even stand to look at a condor or a vulture because they eat dead things. I always say, 'Tell me, sir, do you eat *live* things?' "

Eagles, however, have usually been admired by humans, partly because they look so proud and noble. This is even true of the bald eagle, which doesn't always kill what it eats, but—like the vulture—goes looking for "dead things."

Many nations have put eagles as emblems of strength or nobility on their flags, state buildings, or coins. Certain tribes of American Indians have used eagle feathers as ornaments on their ceremonial robes and headdresses. The bald eagle is the national bird of the United States.

The people who held the birds of prey in the highest esteem before our own time were the falconers. They took advantage of these birds' hunting skills to train them for the sport of falconry. Paintings on ancient tombs and other ruins in Egypt and Asia prove that the sport has been practiced for many centuries.

In falconry a bird of prey is captured when it is young

and is trained to hunt other birds and small mammals for its owner. This was a good way to catch grouse, quail, rabbits, and other game birds and mammals in the days before guns were invented. Once it was trained, the bird of prey could be released to hunt but it would nearly always return to its owner.

Several kinds of birds of prey have been used in the sport of falconry. Golden eagles are sometimes used to hunt larger birds and mammals. The goshawk, a powerful bird of the forest, has also been used in many countries, including the United States. The red-tailed hawk is flown by some falconers. But by far the most popular birds of prey used for hunting are the falcons, for which the sport is named.

Falconry became a favorite pastime for many people during the Middle Ages. Kings and queens, as well as members of the nobility, took part in the sport. The goshawks and some other hawks were not highly regarded because they were often difficult to train, and they were left for people who did not have noble blood. The falcons, which were easier to train and made spectacular dives on their prey from the sky, were kept for the nobles. Kings

The gyrfalcon, a beautiful bird of the far north.

sometimes kept golden eagles for themselves, although they are not as skillful in flight as falcons.

Several kinds of falcons were used in western Europe. For a time the favorite was the largest of the falcons, the gyrfalcon, a beautiful light-colored bird of the far north. The ladies of the court flew small falcons such as the merlin. But gradually over the years the most important bird of falconry became the peregrine. A close examination of this bird of prey makes clear why it is admired by falconers and all those who are thrilled at the sight of a fierce, powerful, and graceful creature in flight.

The peregrine falcon is called by some biologists the world's most successful bird. It lives on all continents and on many of the large chains of oceanic islands. Its name, "peregrine," is traced to a Latin word meaning "wanderer" or "stranger." Its hunting skill allows it to make a good living in the frozen tundra of the north, the rugged inland mountains, the cliffs and beaches along the ocean, the desolate steppes and deserts of Asia, and even crowded, noisy cities.

The settlers who became familiar with this bird of prey in the New World gave it a different name—the duck hawk. Duck hunters often saw the peregrine around their blinds or hiding places on the marshes and beaches and decided that it lived mainly on ducks. This falcon does capture some ducks, but the main attraction those places hold for it is the great stretch of flat, open land where it can easily catch all sorts of birds, such as sandpipers, plovers, small sea birds, and ducks.

The peregrine falcon, in fact, hunts almost any bird that it can strike in midair. It is equipped by nature to be a most deadly hunter of other birds. It is a large-headed bird with fairly long, pointed wings. The adult peregrine is about the size of a crow, or a little larger, and is generally colored slate blue on the back and wings, and pale, almost white, with dark barring, underneath.

The peregrine's crown is dark blue. Its white face is prominently marked on each side with a thick, dark streak, or "mustache." Some people say that the dark streak close to the eyes helps to cut down the glare when it is hunting over water or white beaches, just as a football player puts dark smudges beneath his eyes before going out to play in the bright sun.

The peregrine falcon in its adult plumage is a trim and handsome bird. Its sleek, close-set feathers give it the streamlined form it needs for diving on prey at tremendous speeds from high in the sky. Many other hawks hunt by chasing their prey at low levels over fields or through forests or by dropping a short distance on small birds or mammals that are on the ground. The peregrine sights its prey while it is still at a high altitude and then goes into a steep dive that scientists say may exceed two hundred miles an hour. Slashing through the air with a sound like a rocket, it hits the prey with tremendous force and either kills it on impact or knocks it out of the air.

Like all birds of prey, the peregrine falcon has a sharply hooked beak. But it does not usually kill with its beak. Its deadliest weapons are its powerful yellow feet, tipped with sharp talons. It has four toes on each foot, three in front and one behind. It is that fourth toe, with the sharply curved talon, that slashes the victim in midair and often kills it instantly.

Having struck the prey, the peregrine follows it to the ground. If the prey is still alive, the peregrine kills it by biting it through the spinal cord.

Finally, the peregrine is equipped with keen senses. Few birds have any sense of smell at all, and the peregrine also lacks this sense (among the birds of prey only several kinds of vultures are able to smell, and so can sniff out a rotting carcass). But the peregrine has both excellent hearing and vision. It has huge eyes, and scientists say that the birds of prey probably have sharper eyesight than any other living creature.

A peregrine, flying high on its powerful wings, needs

A peregrine stoops—or dives—at a green-winged teal.

superb vision. As it goes into its steep dive—which falconers call a "stoop"—it must not only pick out its prey from among the flocks of birds below, but it must also time its stoop so that it meets another fast-flying bird at the proper place and angle to make a clean kill.

The British naturalist J. A. Baker once watched a male peregrine stoop from a great height to capture a twisting and dodging sandpiper. Afterward he wrote, "Everything he is has been evolved to link the targeting eye to the striking talon."

3
HAWK MOUNTAIN

Biologists often say that human beings look at animals as if they were characters in a Mother Goose story. We think of them as "good animals" and "bad animals." This view is as silly as if we went around thinking of men and women who eat meat as "bad people" and those who are vegetarians as "good people."

The hatred of hawks goes back for many centuries. We can understand how a farmer would become upset if a hawk got into the barnyard and killed one of his chickens. He might try to shoot that bird if he saw it close to the barnyard again.

But the all-out war against hawks and falcons of all kinds probably was started by European gamekeepers several hundred years ago. In England, for instance, wild animals were considered to be the property of the nobles and other wealthy people who owned the land. These landowners hired gamekeepers to protect the rabbits, grouse, deer, and other birds and mammals that they liked to hunt. They resented other people and predatory animals who came on their property and killed *their* game before they had a chance to hunt it themselves.

The gamekeepers became very efficient at carrying out their employers' orders. If they found poor people from the surrounding towns hunting on the land, they had them arrested. They shot hawks, foxes, and other animals that might bother the game. A common sight in the English countryside was the gibbet, a wooden frame on which gamekeepers hung all the animals they shot, letting them swing and rot in the wind.

Gamekeepers generally developed an intense hatred for the animals they killed. One of the nastiest words in the English language is "vermin"—which usually describes such small and obnoxious pests as rats, lice, and cockroaches. Gamekeepers began to describe even hawks— those beautiful and admirable birds—as vermin.

This hatred of hawks was carried to the New World by European settlers. Hawks often killed "good" birds such as partridge, grouse, and songbirds. So all hawks were simply vermin and fit for nothing but to be shot. This attitude survives even in our own time when certain ignorant people drive up and down highways shooting

16

every hawk they see perched on fence posts or telephone wires.

During the nineteenth century a few people began to speak out against the destruction of hawks. The great American writer Henry David Thoreau admired the flight of hawks and falcons as he watched them from his little cabin on Walden Pond. He believed it was foolish for farmers to kill every hawk because one of them took a chicken occasionally.

"I would rather never taste chickens' meat nor hens' eggs than never to see a hawk sailing through the upper air again," Thoreau wrote. "This sight is worth incomparably more than chicken soup or a boiled egg."

Scientists also began to believe it was foolish to kill hawks, owls, and other predatory birds. They believed this not just because predators are beautiful and exciting creatures that give us pleasure. Their studies showed that in reality most hawks seldom bother barnyard fowl and they have little effect on the populations of game birds such as grouse, pheasant, and ducks. In fact, many kinds of hawks save farmers money by eating large numbers of insects, mice, rats, and other creatures that destroy crops.

But old attitudes are hard to change. Even some well-known naturalists and scientists recognized that most kinds of hawks are good friends to mankind, yet still

17

thought that peregrine falcons were vermin. After all, they reasoned, the peregrine doesn't eat insects or rodents. It kills only other birds, so it must be bad.

One of the best-known defenders of America's wildlife during the first part of the twentieth century was William T. Hornaday, the director of New York City's Bronx Zoo. Hornaday wrote several popular books in which he encouraged his readers to protect wildlife. He helped to get laws passed that gave protection to songbirds, waterfowl, and other species that were threatened by widespread shooting. Yet he drew up a blacklist of birds he believed to be vermin, which included goshawks, Cooper's hawks, sharp-shinned hawks, and golden eagles.

"The peregrine falcon is another hated destroyer of game birds and song birds," Hornaday wrote. "Each bird of this species deserves treatment with a shotgun. First shoot the male and female, then collect the nest, the young or the eggs, whichever may be present. They all look best in collections."

If a conservationist such as Hornaday still felt that way about hawks, it is no wonder that other people clung to their old ideas. Many farmers caught hawks they mistakenly believed were their enemies with pole traps. This is a trap with steel jaws placed on the top of a pole where hawks like to perch. When a hawk lands on a pole, the jaws snap shut, crushing its leg. The hawk hangs

A red-tailed hawk caught in a pole trap, one of the cruelest weapons used against birds of prey.

upside down against the pole, helplessly flapping its wings until it dies or the farmer comes along and kills it.

It became a popular sport to go out into the countryside on weekends and shoot hawks. Since many hunters were not able to tell the difference between a "good" or a "bad" hawk at a distance, they simply shot any large bird of prey they saw.

The slaughter became tremendous as new high-powered guns came on the market. The best time to shoot hawks, the hunters learned, was during the fall migration. As they head south for the winter, hawks of all kinds follow certain flyways that are used every year. Hunters gathered at familiar places such as Cape May, New Jersey, where the birds that fly south along the Atlantic Coast bunch up before crossing Chesapeake Bay. They shot large numbers of peregrine falcons and other hawks at Cape May as they passed on migration.

But perhaps the best-known slaughtering place was a ridge in eastern Pennsylvania that came to be called Hawk Mountain. Every fall thousands of hawks follow the mountain ranges through Pennsylvania on their way south, taking advantage of the air currents there, which make their flight easier. At Hawk Mountain the ridge becomes very narrow and the flights of hawks come together and follow the air currents along the highest section.

For many years hundreds of hunters from all over the

Hawk Mountain

Middle Atlantic states gathered on Hawk Mountain to shoot hawks. It was easy sport. The hawks were very close to the guns as they drifted along the high ridge. Thousands of hawks were killed every fall. In October 1927, a scientist who was studying the plumage of hawks came there and collected 158 hawks of different kinds, all of which had been killed by just a few hunters in a short time.

This was really the only use made of the dead hawks. The hunters just shot them and left them where they fell. If no hawks passed for a while, the hunters shot woodpeckers, jays, and any other birds that came within range.

"The birds are seldom retrieved," wrote a conservationist who visited the mountain, "and I have found many wounded birds still alive after several days."

Why did the hunters come to the mountain to kill hawks? Most of them were not cruel and heartless people. In many cases they had been persuaded by the manufacturers of guns and ammunition that hawk shooting was a valuable service, ridding the world of vermin. The manufacturers made a tidy profit by getting across their message. The hunters often believed they were saving game birds from the "killer hawks." But studies showed there were also large populations of grouse and other game birds on Hawk Mountain, proving that the hawks were taking only a small portion of them.

Reports of the senseless killing aroused people's sympathy for hawks in all parts of the country. Rosalie Edge, who was a prominent conservationist in New York, had the will and the means to do something about the killing. Using her own money, as well as contributions from other people, she bought Hawk Mountain. Then she hired a young naturalist named Maurice Broun to guard the new sanctuary there.

Some people, especially those writing for magazines devoted to hunting, made fun of Rosalie Edge, Maurice Broun, and others who were trying to protect the birds of prey. They could not understand why anyone would protect the "killer hawks." But one of the hawks' most eloquent defenders was a hunter and student of wildlife named Aldo Leopold. He asked people to see the bird of prey as a vital part of the natural world.

"When we attempt to say an animal is 'useful,' 'ugly,' or 'cruel,' we are failing to see it as part of the land," Leopold wrote. "We do not make the same error of calling a carburetor 'greedy.' We see it as a part of a functioning motor."

Meanwhile, Maurice Broun, the guardian of Hawk Mountain, found that he had a hard and dangerous job. Some of the hunters were furious when they were told they could no longer shoot hawks on the mountain. They threatened the lives of Broun and his wife, Irma. But the Brouns held their ground and by their bravery, gentleness, and knowledge stopped the slaughter.

Hawk Mountain

Maurice and Irma Broun won many new friends for the hawks. People came from long distances to see this strange sanctuary devoted to the fierce birds of prey. Some visitors didn't know what to expect. They asked Maurice Broun where the cages were, or they asked Irma Broun, "What time do you feed the hawks?" They thought they were visiting a zoo!

A new day had dawned at Hawk Mountain. Before the Brouns arrived, weekends there had been an uproar of gunfire and shattered wings. Now hundreds of people drove up the rough road to the mountain just for the pleasure of watching those splendid birds drift close overhead on their yearly flight to warmer lands.

4
DEFENDING THE EYRIE

A few government officials began to see that the birds of prey were not vermin but interesting and valuable creatures that deserved a place in our environment. Slowly state laws protecting many birds of prey came into being. In 1934 the Massachusetts legislature passed a law to protect most of the hawks and owls.

It is one thing to pass a law and another thing to enforce it. Ignorant people still shot the large birds of prey when they had a chance. While many birds of prey were still numerous in Massachusetts, there were only a few peregrine falcons left, and state officials knew they would have to make a special effort to protect them.

The Massachusetts state director of fisheries and game gave the job of protecting peregrines to Joseph A. Hagar, the state ornithologist. From a very early time, students of birds were more active in Massachusetts than in any other state. The first state Audubon Society was formed there in 1896 to protect wild birds and their eggs. Hagar, then, had at least some information on the habits and breeding places of Massachusetts peregrines.

Still, the peregrines generally had been considered vermin, and there was not nearly as much information about them as about many other kinds of birds. Even bird students were not willing to make frequent trips to the remote cliffs where peregrines nested—in the days before fast cars and good highways, traveling was often difficult.

But Hagar found records of eleven nesting cliffs in the hills of western Massachusetts, and in March 1935 he set out to visit them. He located ten, as well as four new ones that no one had recorded before. For the next eight years Hagar guarded those nesting cliffs. The reports he brought back added a great deal to our knowledge about the life of the American peregrine falcon.

The nest of a large bird of prey, when it is placed high on a cliff overlooking a wide expanse of valley or the sea, is called an eyrie (usually pronounced "airy"). The eyries chosen by the peregrines in Massachusetts were all somewhat similar. The birds occupied a narrow ledge on a sheer rock face, anywhere from 10 to 130 feet below the very top of the cliff. The eyrie generally overlooked a broad river valley.

Falcon Flight

Hagar has described the breathtaking sight of a pair of these birds at an eyrie on Black Rock. He and one of his helpers were concealed in the woods below the cliff as gale winds tore at the ridge high above them. The male falcon took off into the wind.

"Again and again he started well to leeward and came along the cliff against the wind, diving, plunging, saw-toothing, rolling over and over, darting hither and yon like an autumn leaf until finally he would swoop up into the full current of air and be borne off on the gale to do it all over again."

As Hagar and his companion watched, they marveled at the strength and grace of the falcon, which seemed to play with the relentless force of the wind, dangerously close to the cliff's sharp outcrops.

"At length he tired of this," Hagar wrote of the falcon, "and soaring in narrow circles without any movement of his wings other than a constant small adjustment of their planes, he rose to a position 500 or 600 feet above the mountain and north of the cliff."

For Hagar, as he watched, the grandest moment was still to come.

"Nosing over suddenly, he flicked his wings rapidly 15 or 20 times and fell like a thunderbolt. Wings half closed now, he shot down past the north end of the cliff, described three successive vertical loop-the-loops across

26

The peregrine falcon's beak is sharply hooked for tearing off pieces of flesh after it has killed its prey.

its face, turning completely upside down at the top of each loop, and roared out over our heads with the wind rushing through his wings like ripping canvas. Against the background of the cliff his terrific speed was much more apparent than it would have been in the open sky. The sheer excitement of watching such a performance was tremendous. We felt a strong impulse to stand and cheer."

Hagar made more than a dozen trips a year to most of the eyries. Local fish and game wardens also kept an eye on them as they went about their regular duties, and the state hired several game wardens to help guard eyries where trouble was expected.

The greatest danger did not come from hunters. The eyries were generally high on the cliffs and the slopes below them were thickly wooded, so that few of the birds were shot. As with most other eyries in the northeastern United States at that time, intruders came not to shoot the adult birds, but to rob them of their eggs or young.

What did people want with the eggs of peregrine falcons? At one time there was a craze for collecting the eggs of wild birds. Egg collecting had some scientific value, and naturalists and museum directors made large collections of eggs when they studied the life cycles of birds. Later many amateurs took up collecting eggs just as we might collect stamps, coins, or postcards.

Defending the Eyrie

It is a very destructive hobby, and Audubon societies were originally created to protect the eggs of wild birds as well as the birds themselves. Happily, egg collecting is dying out in the United States, though it is still practiced in Great Britain.

An egg collector did not want simply a single egg from a nest. He wanted the whole clutch—or set—from each nest. Nor did he want simply one set of eggs laid by each species of bird. Ludlow Griscom, a well-known ornithologist in Massachusetts, once told of his visit to a man who had one of the largest egg collections in the United States. The man had 235 sets of robins' eggs. Griscom asked him why he had so many. "That proves that the robin is the commonest nesting bird in this part of the country," the man replied.

The trouble was that the most valuable eggs belonged to the rarest species. Every egg collector wanted sets of peregrine falcon eggs, and they paid high prices for them. No eyrie was safe from collectors. An ornithologist in Pennsylvania some years ago reported that there were four well-known collectors in his part of the state. "Their collections of peregrine eggs are extensive," this man wrote. "There are literally boxes upon boxes of eggs in these collections."

He guessed that egg collectors reduced the population of peregrine falcons in Pennsylvania by at least one third

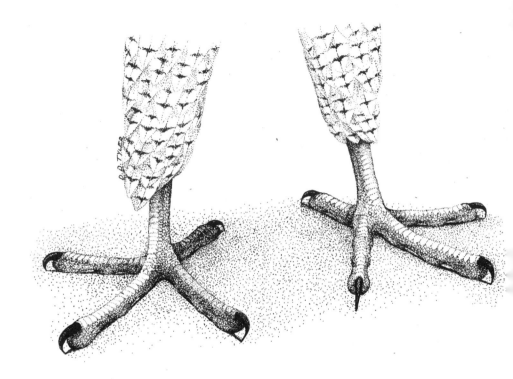

A peregrine usually kills by striking the prey in midair with the curved talons on its heavy yellow feet.

during the 1920s and 1930s. Some of the eyries were so difficult to reach that it took three or four daring climbers, equipped with ropes and other gear, to raid them. A peregrine in that part of the country usually laid four eggs, but if she lost them she laid only three eggs the second time. Sometimes she did not re-lay at all.

Egg collectors carried out their raids all over the United States. Eyries in such states as Connecticut were especially hard hit because they were near large cities. But even eyries along the Potomac River and high into the mountains of West Virginia suffered from collectors. Often the adult falcons were frightened away and did not return to the area.

The other great threat to the eyries was from falconers, who came to take the young birds to be trained for sport. In a sense this practice was even more destructive than egg collecting. A falcon who lost her eggs might lay another clutch, but if her chicks were stolen she would not raise another brood that year.

Still, guarding the eyries was a rewarding job for Joseph Hagar. As he watched, day after day, he was privileged to learn the courting and nesting secrets of one of the world's most fascinating birds.

5

THE TERCEL AND
THE FALCON

A cold wind blew through the valley. It swirled over the
farms, which were still splotched here and there with
snow, and swept the rock face of the cliffs above. A male
peregrine perched on the dead branch of a leafless tree
that clung to the cliff's face. It seemed that both the tree
and the lone bird would be carried away in the sweep of
wind from the west.

But the peregrine, his close-set feathers hardly ruffled
by the gale, was intent on something else. He faced the
wind, cocking his blunt head this way and that as he
searched the sky. Finally his gaze focused on a dot against
the gray clouds a great distance away. The peregrine
watched as the dot drew closer, expanding now into a
familiar shape—a blunt-headed, short-tailed bird flying
with rapid beats of its long, sickle-shaped wings. The

peregrine had recognized the newcomer as one of his own kind.

The newcomer was a female peregrine falcon flying from the south into an early New England March. The male bird had been perched near the cliff for a week or more, waiting for such a sight. As the newcomer drew near, the male became more agitated and launched himself into the air. He flew back and forth across the cliff's face, uttering again and again a call that sounded like the turning of a rusty hinge. "We-chew! We-chew!"

At first the newcomer paid no attention. She flew quickly past the cliff. The male bird redoubled his efforts. "We-chew! We-chew!" he called as he swooped up the face of the cliff and plunged down again against the wind in a spectacular exhibition of his flying skill. He was displaying for the newcomer the expanse of cliff. He was drawing attention to the splendid eyrie. He was inviting her to join him there.

"We-chew! We-chew!" he called.

The newcomer began to show some interest in the pleading call from the cliff. Folding her dark wings, she plunged like a great feathered rock. As she approached the cliff, she opened her wings, slowed her fall, and lightly rose again onto a rocky ledge where the other peregrine had already landed.

This was the opening of a drama that was played out

every spring for thousands of years on cliffs all over the United States. It was the courtship and mating of peregrine falcons as they prepared to raise young birds that would carry on their kind.

Every naturalist who was fortunate enough to watch the peregrines at an eyrie speaks of his own sense of excitement. This is the emotion stirred in an audience by all great performers, and in a way the peregrines at an eastern eyrie were great performers. But the performance they put on was not meant for human eyes. The aerial displays, the piercing calls, and all the rest were acts developed by the birds through ages and ages of time to persuade each other to carry out this most important act of their lives.

The two peregrines on the ledge were well fitted by nature for the task that lay ahead of them. Although the female peregrine was four years old, two years younger than the male, she was much the larger of the two. From the tip of her hooked beak to her squared-off tail she measured twenty-one inches, while he was barely over fifteen inches long. In fact falconers always call the male peregrine a "tercel"—a name that is traced back to the Latin word for "third." The tercel is about one third smaller than the female, which falconers simply call a falcon.

Why is the falcon larger than the tercel? In other

species, including human beings, the male is generally larger than the female. Ornithologists have argued about this difference in peregrines for a long time, and they seem to have come up with a good explanation.

Tom J. Cade, a falconer and ornithologist, says that these large hawks are naturally so fierce, so predatory, and—for most of the year—so solitary in their way of life that it is hard for them to be sociable when it comes time to mate. The tercel takes the most forceful role in mating. If he were the larger of the pair, the combination of size and forcefulness might be too much for the falcon and frighten her away.

The falcon on the rocky ledge was still suspicious of the tercel beside her. He had yet to prove his good intentions. The next morning he flew off across the valley. Climbing on his strong wings, he reached a great height, from which he had a wide view of the air space below. Within half an hour he flew back toward the ledge, carrying a blue jay in the talons of one powerful yellow foot. He had made a kill.

The falcon was instantly alert. She left the little tree where she had been waiting and flew out to meet the tercel. As he swooped over her, he dropped the jay. The falcon rolled over in the air and, flying upside down, extended her foot and caught the falling jay. Then she returned to her tree with the dead bird. Holding it against

the branch with one foot, she swiftly plucked the jay, its feathers drifting off in the wind, and then began to eat it.

The tercel watched from the nearby ledge. The falcon had accepted his gift, and in effect she had accepted him. The two peregrines were now a pair. The falcon had been attracted by the tercel, whose old mate had been killed during the previous year. These two peregrines were paired for life and would join each other at this cliff each year until one of them died and the other found a new mate.

The tercel often brought back dead birds to his mate. At other times they hunted over the valley together. No matter which one made the kill, the falcon always ate the first bird they caught. Joseph A. Hagar has recalled how a falcon he was watching captured a pigeon. He described the pursuit as thrilling to watch, but also blood-chilling:

"The pigeon had been flying level and at top speed. The falcon had been descending slightly with strong, rapid wing-beats and was moving at least twice as fast as the pigeon, so that the gap between them closed with speed.

"In the instant before the strike, the falcon had arrived

A peregrine perches near its eyrie on the face of a steep cliff, waiting for its mate to return.

at a point perhaps 12 feet behind the pigeon and a foot below it, when she suddenly changed direction, extended her talons, shot up across the pigeon's back, and, at the moment of passing, grappled her prey, apparently by the body just behind the wings, so that the two birds swept on as one without the least pause. One instant the pigeon was flying desperately. The very next, it hung a limp bundle, with drooping wings and neck, in the talons of its terrible pursuer."

Day by day the tercel's excitement continued to rise. As the falcon watched from the tree, he put on his spectacular aerial displays. Often the tercel ended his courtship flight by landing on a ledge in the cliff's face. Then he would scrape the loose soil and gravel with his feet and break out in his familiar, wailing call, inviting the falcon to the eyrie.

For a time the falcon paid no attention. She needed to be coaxed. But one day she followed the tercel to the ledge. There the two peregrines scratched together in the soil and loose rock and called to each other in creaky tones. The falcon then flew back to her perch in the little tree.

After one of those visits to the ledge, the tercel flew to the tree with her, mounted her back, and mated with her. From then on they mated several times a day. They also perched together on the tree or a ledge, where they preened their feathers, cleaning and straightening them by running them one by one through their beaks. The falcon liked to preen the hard-to-reach feathers on the tercel's neck.

The falcon began to catch some of the tercel's sense of excitement now. She visited various ledges on the cliff. She flew from one to the other, scratching around in the loose rock and looking closely at her surroundings. Finally she picked out one of the ledges. It may have been the tercel's cliff, but the falcon selected the ledge that was to be their eyrie.

The falcon began to spend much of her time on that ledge. Peregrines differ from most other kinds of birds— they do not build a true nest. The falcon simply scraped away some of the loose rock on the ledge and made a shallow depression in the thin layer of soil. She moved her body around in the depression, widening and smoothing it.

The eyrie was ready for the next stage in the drama.

6
FAMILY LIFE

The falcon laid her first egg early in April. The egg was a handsome object in itself. It was slightly smaller and rounder than a chicken's egg. The underlying color of the shell was grayish-white. But nearly hiding this basic color was a dense spatter of rich brown and reddish spots.

The falcon did not begin to incubate her egg at once. It lay unprotected on the ledge in the center of the small scrape, twelve inches across, that the peregrine had made with her talons and body. Around it on the ledge was the eyrie's litter—flakes of rock, a broken twig, and slivers of bird bones left from the falcon's recent meals.

Two days later she laid another egg, and after two more days she laid a third. Only then did the falcon settle down over her eggs in the scrape and begin to incubate them. She laid a fourth egg two days later to complete her clutch.

Each egg was a compact package of life and food.

Family Life

Growing inside was an embryo—a tiny organism that would absorb nourishment from the rich mass of food around it and eventually grow into a fully formed peregrine chick. When the peregrine laid her first eggs, she was able to slow the growth of the embryos by not warming—or incubating—them. When her clutch was nearly completed she began incubating. Thus the embryos all started to grow again at the same time and the chicks would hatch in fairly close sequence.

For many weeks now the peregrine would be confined to the narrow ledge. There, under a warm sun or a driving rain, she would shelter the eggs with her body. Small areas of naked skin called brood patches developed on the underside of her plumage. Blood vessels ran close to the surface of her body at those places and she kept her eggs especially warm when she fitted them to the brood patches.

The falcon seldom left the eyrie once she started incubating her eggs. The tercel did most of the hunting. He ranged out across the valley searching for prey— usually small birds such as swallows and finches that he could carry back easily to his mate. When the falcon saw him coming, carrying a dead bird in the long curved talons of one foot, she flew from the eyrie to meet him. He passed the prey to her and she carried it to the little tree, where she plucked and ate it. The tercel took over her place, incubating the eggs until she finished eating.

41

Four weeks passed. The clouds of early spring scattered and the warm sun of May shone down on the eyrie. These were quiet days for the peregrines. The falcon sat on her eggs, dozing sometimes or watching passing birds and insects. The tercel perched on the dead limb of the tree when he wasn't hunting and alertly guarded the eyrie. If another bird approached too near—even one as large as a great horned owl or an eagle—he rushed at it fiercely, hastening the startled intruder on its way.

One day the falcon heard faint sounds beneath her. Her chicks, fully formed now in the dark of the eggs, were beginning to chirp. Sometimes the falcon clucked softly in response. She was assured by the chirping that life existed down there under the warm mass of her feathers.

The shells of her eggs were beginning to weaken with age and the constant pressure of her body. As she began to feel movement within the eggs, her own attention was focused more and more on them. She refused to leave the scrape now even to eat.

Inside the eggs the chicks had grown a sharp scalelike tip to the upper beak called an egg tooth. By instinct the chicks began to tap the shell lining with the egg tooth, weakening it still further. At last a star-shaped crack appeared in one of the shells. Pipping by fits and starts, a chick shattered the eggshell and it fell apart.

The tiny creature that tumbled out into the scrape

looked barely alive. The sparse fuzz that covered it was still wet and matted. Its head seemed too large for its body and especially for its scrawny neck, so that the chick lay sprawled full length, its chin flat on the scrape.

But the chick dried quickly. Its covering of short, creamy-white down fluffed out. The falcon cleared a place for the chick beneath her by dropping the empty eggshell off the ledge. She had to shelter the chick with her body just as she covered the eggs because the thin down would not protect it on chilly nights or windy days.

Within a couple of days there were three chicks in the eyrie. Something had gone wrong in the fourth egg and it never hatched. At first the chicks seemed very feeble. Their legs were too weak to stand on and their bleary eyes seemed to make out little but shadowy shapes in the new world around them. They sat up unsteadily, with their pale feet thrust out in front of them.

Yet the chicks kept their parents busy. They were always hungry, and their pleading cries were amazingly loud. The tercel flew over the valley, stooping at small birds and killing them with a blow of his deadly talons. The falcon flew from the eyrie on his return and took the dead bird to the tree where she plucked the feathers from it. Then she flew back to the eyrie. The parents were good providers. The falcon tore thin strips of flesh from the prey and let them hang from her bill so that the chicks

A falcon broods its chick at the eyrie, keeping it warm until thicker plumage grows and replaces its thin coat of down.

could snatch them and swallow them hungrily. Sometimes she fed her chicks a sliver of bone to give them calcium.

The chicks grew incredibly fast. Although they weighed only one ounce when they hatched, they weighed about six ounces a week later and more than ten ounces a few weeks after that. By this time a longer, thicker down had replaced their earlier covering and the creamy-white color had darkened to pale gray on their backs.

When the chicks were about three weeks old, the dark, stiff flight feathers were beginning to poke through the down on the wings and tail. Their legs were stronger now. They stood up when the falcon came to the eyrie and scrambled madly for their food.

After a month great changes became apparent in the chicks. Their feathers were growing and beginning to give their bodies the shape of adult peregrines. The head and back had darkened, with only patches of down showing through, and the mustache stripes were clear now on their faces.

They were nearly as large as adults. They were so strong and they squabbled so ferociously over food that the adults no longer fed them individually. They simply passed over the ledge, dropping the prey to the squeaking chicks, and flew on.

The chicks in their cliffside eyrie were perfectly safe from animal predators. No bird or beast would face the

The peregrine chick is unable to stand on its weak legs for some time after it hatches.

raking talons of the watchful adults to get at them. Only humans, with their ropes and cleated boots, could reach the ledge.

The greatest danger to the chicks came from their own increasing activity. During the lively struggles over food on the ledge, barely two or three feet wide in places, there was always the possibility that one of the chicks would be knocked over the edge and fall to its death on the rocks below.

The chicks were also beginning to exercise their wings. Facing into the wind, they flapped their wings vigorously, sometimes jumping several inches upward from the ledge as if on a practice flight. If a strong gust of wind swept the ledge at that moment, it could carry an unwary chick off before it was truly ready to fly.

At five weeks old the young peregrines were finally strong enough to leave the eyrie. Plenty of food and their own exercises had strengthened their wing muscles. Now, instead of dropping food for them on the ledge, the parents flew rapidly past, the prey dangling from their talons. It was as if they were daring the screaming young to fly. When the young birds, wanting to fly but still cautious, remained on the ledge, the adults would turn back and drop them their food.

In the middle of June the eldest of the young peregrines, a male, accepted the dare. He launched himself into space and at once was speeding out across the valley as if he had been flying for years. The falcon rose above him and dropped her prey. The young tercel snatched it from the air with his talons and flew with it to the little tree. There, holding it to the branch with one heavy foot, he began to tear off strips of the prey's flesh as he had learned to do at the eyrie.

Soon all three young peregrines were flying. They still depended on their parents to supply them with food, but they were sharpening their own skills. Time and again they gave chase to smaller birds or stooped at them from the clouds with great speed though uncertain aim. By the end of the summer their parents had disappeared, but the skillful young peregrines had become hunters on their own.

They too set off on migration to the south, just as peregrines had for thousands of years. But these peregrines and many others hatched that spring were different. Although outwardly they looked as powerful as any of their race that had gone before them, they carried in their bodies the mysterious poison that was to put an end to this fascinating drama in vast areas of the United States and Europe.

7
THE MYSTERY OF
THE PEREGRINES

The peregrine falcon, as we wrote earlier, is called the most successful bird in the world. It is a marvelous flier—swift, powerful, and graceful. It is a skillful hunter, striking other fast-flying birds from the sky with a single blow of its curved talons. Races of the peregrine falcon are found almost everywhere in the world—from the Arctic tundra, isolated mountains, and rocky seacoasts, to scorching deserts. Yet nowhere are these birds numerous. Scientists say that there were never more than one thousand nesting pairs of peregrines at any one time in the United States south of Alaska.

There are several reasons for this scarcity. Although in some regions peregrines have taken over large holes or nests left in trees by other birds, in many places it nests only on ledges or in small caves high in cliff faces—

which are hard to find. A cliff can only be used by a single pair of peregrines because they will not allow other peregrines to nest near by.

During the nesting season a peregrine must also have a wide open area in which to hunt. Its manner of hunting —stooping from great heights at birds it finds in the open—is not effective in thickly forested areas, where the prey can fly for cover among the trees.

A peregrine also needs a large supply of the right kind of prey during the nesting season. The smaller tercel, which does most of the hunting at that time, must kill birds that are light enough to carry long distances to the eyrie. The best prey are pigeons, sandpipers, small sea birds, and other species that fly out over open spaces in large numbers.

These needs of the nesting peregrine are not always easily met in one place. For many years one of the best-known and most successful group of eyries in the eastern United States was located in the cliffs along the lower Hudson River, near New York City. There, close to millions of people, the peregrines found all the right natural conditions for nesting, including a large supply of pigeons.

In fact, peregrine falcons were learning to take advantage of our own liking for living and working in high places. They began to make their eyries on the ledges of skyscrapers, churches, and other large buildings in cities all over the world. The most famous of these birds was called the "Sun Life Falcon." She nested in Montreal for sixteen years on the headquarters of the Sun Life Assurance Company of Canada. During those years she had three different mates and raised a total of twenty-one young.

Unfortunately, the people of New York City were not as kind to the peregrines that came to nest on their skyscrapers. Some people were afraid of the birds. A pair that nested on a ledge of the fashionable St. Regis Hotel in midtown Manhattan stooped on hotel guests who used the penthouse above the eyrie. The birds were captured with nets and removed.

Many people keep and train pigeons in cities. In New York these pigeon handlers especially hated peregrines. A pair of peregrines hatched eleven young in the years 1943 through 1948 on New York skyscrapers but not one of them fledged—or flew away from—the eyrie alive. Some were taken by falconers. The others, because of the hatred for these hawks, were killed by the American Society for the Prevention of Cruelty to Animals.

During those years the eyries along the lower Hudson River were carefully watched by Richard A. Herbert and his wife, Kathleen Skelton Herbert, who were interested in the peregrines' welfare. In three eyries carefully checked by the Herberts from 1943 through 1948, the peregrines hatched thirty-three young. Three died in the eyries. Falconers took eighteen young and twelve others left the eyries on their own. Those were the most successful of the eight eyries watched every year by the Herberts. All of the eyries were producing at least some young. But in 1950 disaster struck these peregrines.

A number of the eyries the Herberts watched were on the New Jersey side of the river in Palisades Park. In 1950 construction was started on the Palisades Interstate Parkway. Workmen used bulldozers on the cliffs to clear away trees and dynamite to clear away rocks. The Palisades Park was supposed to be a wildlife refuge, but work on the parkway certainly upset the peregrines' nesting patterns.

That was at a time before the federal government required the builders of highways and other large projects to prepare an Environmental Impact Statement. In these statements the builders must report how they are going to go about building the project and show whether the benefits of their method outweigh the environmental damage. The cliffs might not have been disturbed so badly if the builders had laid out the parkway in a different manner.

In any case the Herberts discovered that in 1950—for

the first time in history—no young were hatched in the eight eyries along the lower Hudson River. The Herberts blamed this on the parkway builders and the very cold weather that spring.

But in 1951 only two young were hatched along the Hudson. One of them was taken from the eyrie by a falconer from Brooklyn. They were the last young peregrines ever hatched in those eyries.

For some years after that, Richard and Kathleen Herbert kept visiting the eyries during the nesting season. They saw the birds trying to nest, but without success. Sometimes the falcons laid eggs, but the eggs never hatched. They disappeared or broke in the eyrie. Finally the adult peregrines did not even show up in the spring. In 1959, when they visited all the eyries, the Herberts saw only one peregrine.

After that they were gone. The peregrines even stopped coming into New York City during the winter to capture pigeons and starlings. The Herberts decided that human beings had driven the peregrines from the eyries. The eyrie-robbing falconers and the visitors brought to Palisades Park by the new parkway seemed to have been too much for the peregrines.

But Joseph A. Hagar was having a similar experience at the remote eyries in western Massachusetts. One of the

Pigeons, which are called rock doves when they breed in the wild, used to draw many peregrines to major cities.

eyries he visited regularly was on a cliff over the Quabbin Reservoir. Locked gates two or three miles away kept the public from the reservoir, and so the peregrines were not disturbed by human beings. In 1946 Hagar's studies showed that the eyrie at Quabbin, as well as those elsewhere in the state, were more successful than ever.

The very next year the good news changed to bad. The peregrines raised few young. Each year at Quabbin and other eyries, Hagar found that the eggs did not hatch or were quickly broken. He had rarely ever found broken eggs in the eyries before. Once in a while a chick hatched, but it soon died.

In 1950 the falcon at Quabbin laid five eggs. Four of them broke and the other disappeared. Hagar saw the tracks of a raccoon near the eyrie and thought that the animal was smashing the eggs. Within a year or two the adult peregrines no longer tried to nest. The Massachusetts eyries were abandoned.

No one realized exactly what was happening. A few bird students such as Richard and Kathleen Herbert and Joseph Hagar noticed that the falcons in their areas had stopped nesting. But each thought that the trouble was only local. Each thought that the trouble was caused only by falconers, highway builders, or raccoons.

Many of these stories reached Joseph J. Hickey, an ornithologist at the University of Wisconsin. Back in 1940 he had made a survey and discovered there were 275 peregrine eyries in the United States east of the Rocky Mountains. He decided that a new survey was needed to find out exactly what was happening. In 1964, ornithologists cooperated in making a survey of all the eyries in the eastern United States, and they found that all of them had been abandoned by the peregrines.

The ornithologists were stunned. Nothing quite like this had ever happened before. Ornithologists knew that the peregrines faced many dangers in the modern world, but none had dreamed that an entire population—at remote mountain eyries as well as near large cities— would entirely disappear. It was an almost unbelievable disaster.

At that moment, across the ocean, a British scientist was beginning to unravel the mystery.

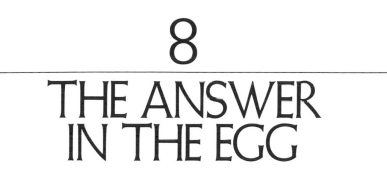

8

THE ANSWER
IN THE EGG

Derek A. Ratcliffe is one of Great Britain's experts on the lives of falcons and other birds of prey. Because he was alert to certain environmental changes in Britain, he was able to carry out the skillful scientific detective work that shed light on the dangers that birds faced in many parts of the world.

For hundreds of years human beings persecuted peregrine falcons in Britain. Gamekeepers shot them whenever they had the chance. Egg collectors robbed their nests. During World War II the British armed forces shot many peregrines because they ate the carrier pigeons that were used to send messages between army units.

But the peregrines always found ways to survive. After the war they went on raising young in their isolated eyries and their population climbed back to normal. Then, in the 1950s, the population began to drop.

Scientists like Ratcliffe were puzzled. They studied

57

many possible causes for the peregrines' decline, but none of them seemed to fit the case. When Ratcliffe visited the eyries, he saw that peregrines were trying to raise young, but with little success. The eggs were breaking in the eyries. Often the falcons were eating their own eggs.

Ratcliffe collected the broken shells from some of those eyries. Like a detective, he was looking for clues. The eggshells felt extremely thin and fragile to him. Then Ratcliffe had one of those inspirations that sometimes bring about a breakthrough in scientific studies. He remembered all of those sets of eggs collected from eyries in the past.

Ratcliffe began a series of experiments. With the aid of delicate measuring instruments developed by the poultry industry, he measured the thickness of the peregrines' eggs he had found in old collections. Then he measured the shells he had recently gathered in the unsuccessful eyries. The new shells were much thinner than the old ones, sometimes by as much as 25 percent.

Now Ratcliffe realized that something was interfering with the peregrines' ability to form eggshells. At the same time, British scientists discovered that golden eagles in western Scotland were having the same problem. Many of those eagles did not even lay eggs anymore. Nearly half of the eagles that did lay eggs broke them in the nest. Yet the golden eagles that lived in the central Highlands of Scotland had no such problems raising their young.

The Answer in the Egg

What made the difference? The eagles that were in trouble lived in a sheep-raising area. To protect their flocks from maggots, the growers dipped them in a liquid that contained one of the long-lasting chemical poisons called pesticides that were developed right after World War II. Eagles often fed on the carcasses of sheep that died in the pastures.

The eagles that lived in the central Highlands preyed on grouse. The grouse ate mostly heather, which was not sprayed with pesticides. Derek Ratcliffe began to put all this information together. He noticed, for instance, that the great decline in the numbers of peregrines started just after the long-lasting pesticides such as DDT began to be used widely by British farmers. He also noticed that the decline of the peregrines and some other birds of prey started a few years earlier in the United States—just when those pesticides were first put into use.

Ratcliffe sent the results of his experiments on eggshells to Joseph J. Hickey at the University of Wisconsin. Hickey immediately made his own experiments, using eggs from old collections and those taken recently from unsuccessful eyries in the United States. Like Ratcliffe, he found the new shells much thinner than the old ones.

Was DDT the cause of the peregrines' disappearance? Soon many scientists were at work on the problem. Some of them fed DDT in small amounts to kestrels, ducks, and other common birds in laboratory experiments. They

Peregrine falcons killed and ate many smaller birds that were already contaminated with DDT. In that way they built up harmful amounts of the poison in their own bodies.

60

found that those birds laid eggs with thinner shells than usual or that their young died.

Naturalists discovered that several other species of large American birds were in serious trouble. The bald eagle disappeared from several parts of the country. The osprey—the great fish hawk of our rivers and bays—laid eggs that did not hatch. Brown pelicans crushed their eggs as they tried to incubate them.

Scientists also learned that all species of birds were not affected in the same way by DDT. Some falcons, such as the American kestrel and the prairie falcon, were not disappearing like the peregrine. Even the populations of peregrines showed important differences for a while. The peregrines in the northeastern United States were gone, but those races that lived in the Arctic or the Far West seemed to be holding their own.

Finally, scientists were able to solve the mystery of the peregrines. When DDT and other long-lasting pesticides were sprayed on crops to kill pest insects, they did not simply break down and disappear. These poisons remained in the environment for many years, though often at low levels. These low levels were absorbed by many tiny creatures—other insects, worms, and small fish.

The long-lasting pesticides, then, got into living food chains. Birds and larger fish that ate many of the small creatures began to build up larger amounts of DDT in

their bodies. As this food chain continued, the largest predators began to store harmful amounts of DDT in their bodies.

Sometimes the stored DDT killed them. More often it caused harmful changes in their bodies. Certain birds, such as peregrines and bald eagles, that ate many smaller birds or fish were no longer able to produce enough of the female hormone called estrogen. The females of these species could not carry out the proper nesting steps. They did not provide their eggs with the calcium to form strong shells.

Could anything be done to save these birds? Professor Hickey, with the help of money supplied by organizations such as the National Audubon Society, called a conference at the University of Wisconsin in 1966. Experts on birds of prey gathered there from all over the world. They talked about the troubles of these birds in their own regions.

The story that came out of the conference was an alarming one. In regions of the United States and northern Europe where DDT and the other long-lasting pesticides had been used for a long time, the peregrine

---

Scientists used the kestrel, a small falcon, in laboratory experiments to test the effects of DDT on the eggs of birds of prey.

63

was gone or nearly gone. In other places, where those poisons had not been used much as yet, the peregrines were still healthy.

But as the new methods of agriculture and forestry were brought to less developed nations, mankind's use of these poisons increased. They were even being carried by winds and ocean currents to places where DDT was never used. There were signs that peregrines in remote Arctic and mountainous regions were also beginning to have trouble raising their young.

Some experts believed it was already too late to save the peregrines. It would be difficult to change the new methods of agriculture. They said that even if farmers stopped using DDT and turned to less harmful pesticides, DDT would remain in the world's environment for many years to come. The peregrines would disappear before DDT did.

But a few scientists and conservationists refused to give up hope. The National Audubon Society joined with other groups in trying to have the use of DDT stopped. By 1973 the federal government had banned nearly all uses of DDT in this country. Several other nations did the same thing. The peregrine still had a slim chance.

9
FALCONERS

One of the most difficult questions that modern biologists must answer is whether to save wild animals from extinction by breeding them in captivity.

Some people argue against this plan. They say it is wrong to take animals from the wild and lock them up in cages—especially if there are very few of them left. They say that nature should take its course. All animals will ultimately become extinct, and if an animal species cannot survive in the modern world, human beings should not interfere. Let the doomed animal live out its last days with dignity in the wild.

Other people hold a different opinion. They say that these animals are not becoming extinct through natural causes, but by the carelessness, violence, and modern technology of humans. These people believe that we ought to take a few animals from endangered populations and breed them in captivity. Then, when the dangerous situations are corrected, we can release them so that they may start a new population in the wild.

There were good reasons for accepting this second view in the case of the peregrine falcon. A program to breed peregrines had an important advantage because there was a group of men in North America who already had much experience handling these birds in captivity. They were the falconers.

It is one thing to keep peregrines in captivity for sport and quite another thing to get two of them to breed and raise young birds. There were scientists and conservationists who thought it could not be done. Peregrines are too wild, they said. They will not mate without going through their strenuous courtship flights in the wild.

Heinz Meng is a falconer who believed it was possible. He knew that another falconer had mated two peregrines and reared chicks in wartime Germany. It was very difficult, but the possibility was there.

Meng had studied birds at Cornell University. He had also become a falconer, training hawks and falcons of different kinds to hunt and then return to him. After he became a professor of biology at the State University of New York at New Paltz, he began to study birds of prey more closely. He often watched peregrines at their eyries in the nearby mountains. Although he was a falconer, he did not take young birds from the eyrie. He captured his falcons with traps on beaches during the fall migration.

When the falcons finally disappeared from the northeastern United States, he decided to try to get his own peregrines to breed. Because of his experience, he was able to handle them without making them nervous. You have to think like a bird to be able to work with them, Meng says—you have to be a "bird brain."

Meng built a special house for his peregrines. For six years he tried to get them to mate, but with no success. The birds were too wild.

Fortunately there were other peregrine falcons available. The peregrines of North America are divided into three large subspecies, or races. Separation into several subspecies occurs often in a species that covers a vast area. The different subspecies live in their own areas and seldom have contact with each other. Where these areas meet, the different subspecies will sometimes breed with each other. After long periods of time, if the subspecies grow so different that they can no longer communicate and breed with each other, they will become separate species.

Scientists gave names to the American peregrine's three subspecies. The map of North America on page 70

D.D.TYLER

shows where these subspecies live:
- In the far north lives the peregrine of the tundra—that partly frozen, treeless land where only stunted shrubs and small plants grow. Scientists call this subspecies *tundrius*.
- South of the tundra, across part of Canada, through the western United States, and down into Mexico, lives the subspecies that scientists call *anatum*. This name is related to the Latin word for "duck" and refers to the bird's original name, duck hawk.
- Along the coasts of Oregon and Washington, British Columbia, southwestern Alaska, and out onto the Aleutian Islands, lives the Peale's peregrine, or *pealei*, a subspecies named for an early American naturalist.

Heinz Meng spoke to several falconers on the West Coast about his attempts to breed peregrines. These falconers captured two young peregrines at eyries in Canada's Queen Charlotte Islands and sent them to Meng. They were from the subspecies called Peale's peregrines, and of course they had no real experience in the wild.

Meng put them in his hawk house at New Paltz. This building had perches and a ledge that the peregrines

A peregrine perches on the falconer's thick leather glove, where it is held by leg straps called jesses.

TUNDRIUS

ANATUM

PEALEI

FORMER BREEDING
RANGE

WINTER RANGE

This is a map of North America, showing where the three subspecies, or races, of the peregrine falcon breed.

Tundrius, *the peregrine of the tundra, breeds in the far north.* Anatum, *the duck hawk, breeds south of the tundra and in the western United States.* Pealei, *named for an early naturalist, breeds in a smaller area on the West Coast.*

could use for an eyrie. Finally, when these birds were four years old, they began to show signs of courting.

The tercel considered the hawk house his breeding territory. He threatened Meng even when the falconer brought the birds their food. Acting like a bird to try to give the tercel confidence, Meng cowered before him as if he were frightened. He dropped the peregrines' food and left hurriedly.

The falcon laid her eggs on the ledge Meng had built for her. One day when Meng approached the ledge, the tercel flew at him, knocked his cap off, and flew away with it to the other side of the room. The tercel was being a protective father.

In 1971 the captive peregrines hatched their first chick. Meng named it Prince Philip. It was a good name for the chick because his Canadian parents were from the British Commonwealth, the peregrine was a bird of "noble" rank, and the real Prince Philip is a well-known conservationist.

The section marked with dots in the eastern and central United States shows where a population of the subspecies anatum *bred before DDT wiped it out. The slanting lines in the southern United States and Mexico show where many of the far northern birds spend the winter. They sometimes fly as far as South America on migration.*

71

Soon Meng and other falconers were breeding more peregrine chicks in captivity. The chances for building a new peregrine population in the northeastern United States had once seemed dim. Now, the first important step was taken, but years of hard and imaginative work lay ahead before a few captive chicks could be bred into a healthy wild population.

The job was too big for one falconer or even a small group of falconers. In 1973 Heinz Meng sent his birds to Cornell University at Ithaca, New York. From now on Cornell would be the headquarters for the exciting new Peregrine Project.

10
PEREGRINE PALACE

In 1970 a letter arrived at Cornell's Laboratory of Ornithology. It had been written by two boys named Orin Starn and Jay Hart in Berkeley, California, and with it was a gift of two dollars. The letter read:

"Me and my Friend have been studying birds, especially the Peregrine Falcon. One day he came over and showed me a newspaper article about you trying to save the Peregrine, so we have been going around collecting money to help your project. I hope everything works out alright."

This was the first contribution to the Peregrine Fund, which supports the program to bring the peregrines back to those parts of the United States and Canada where they had once ruled the skies. The Massachusetts Audubon Society followed with a large gift. A number of people, as well as organizations such as the National

Audubon Society, local Audubon chapters, and clubs
devoted to the birds of prey, all gave generously to the
fund. (Those who donate a thousand dollars become
"godparents" to a pair of breeding peregrines and receive
an invitation to visit them and have a detailed report on
their progress.)

From these beginnings rose one of the most remarkable
birdhouses in the world. It is a large, barnlike building,
227 feet long and 47 feet wide. It has an aluminum roof,
with its sides open to the weather and covered by bars
and wire screen. The building is divided into forty
chambers, each of them 18 feet high at the peak. A pair
of adult peregrines lives in each chamber.

Tom Cade, who directs the Peregrine Project, spoke of
his hopes after the breeding program was underway at
Cornell:

"No doubt some of the same people who have been
saying that captive breeding of the peregrine is imprac-
tical because of the great difficulty will now be the ones
to begin deriding our efforts to put captive-bred falcons
in nature. They will say, 'impossible.' Proving them
wrong again will be an exciting challenge. We believe
there will be free-flying and breeding peregrines in some
of their old haunts in the eastern United States by 1980."

Cade (who is an expert falconer himself) and his
helpers benefitted from the work being done by other
American and Canadian falconers. By 1973 they had four

pairs of breeding peregrines in their building, which they nicknamed "Peregrine Palace." Great care had to be taken at every step. Through bitter experience Cade learned that even the slightest mistake would keep the eggs from hatching or cause the chicks to die.

The project would be successful only if Cade and his helpers were able to rear a large number of peregrines. All species of birds suffer heavy losses during their first year of life in the wild. Many peregrines had to be released to make up for the losses expected from predators, accidents, disease, and human troublemakers. To raise peregrines at Cornell, Cade combined the best techniques of falconry and the poultry industry.

A chamber at Peregrine Palace is a breeding pair's territory. It is furnished with short perches, which are tree limbs attached to the wall. It also has several nesting ledges on the walls, each about four feet wide—the most popular, as far as the birds are concerned, being about fourteen feet above the gravel-covered floor. The center of the chamber is kept free for flying.

The ornithologist working with the peregrines can watch them without being seen by standing outside the chamber in a corridor that runs through the building's center. They watch through an opening covered by one-way glass. The peregrines will remain "wilder" if they have little contact with humans.

The adults live in the chamber year round. If the falcon

becomes too aggressive toward the tercel, she is tied to her perch by jesses—a pair of leather straps fastened to her legs that falconers use in holding their birds. Otherwise, at certain times of the year the falcon might kill the smaller tercel.

The workers feed the peregrines through a door in the wall. The meals are made up of freshly killed birds and animals that are raised for that purpose—chickens, quail, rats, and rabbits. As breeding time approaches, the diet is changed somewhat to help the peregrines establish their "pair bond"—to become closer together. They are given small quail several times a day. This diet allows the tercel to go through the ceremony of plucking its "prey" and giving it to the falcon.

Once breeding begins, Peregrine Palace becomes something of an egg factory. Tom Cade and his helpers allow the falcon to incubate her eggs for a week. Then they remove the eggs from the ledge and put them in a small forced-air incubator. The incubator is kept at about 98° Fahrenheit, with a relative humidity of about 40 percent. Workers turn the eggs four to eight times each day—just as the falcon would do at the eyrie—to keep the embryos from sticking to the shells.

Meanwhile, after about two weeks the falcon moves to another ledge in the chamber and lays a second clutch of eggs. These eggs are also removed to incubators seven days later.

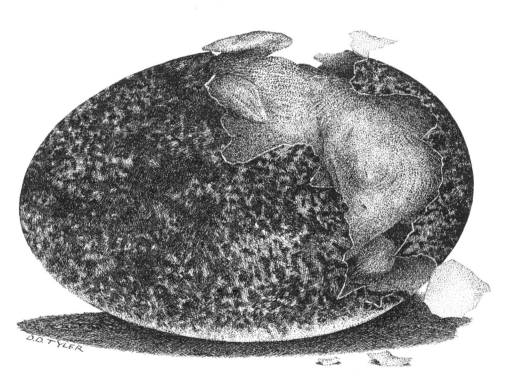

Young men and women at Cornell carefully watch the handsomely marked falcon eggs in incubators. It is an exciting moment when a chick begins to hatch.

When the eggs begin to hatch, they are placed in a piece of equipment called a hatcher. On the average, three out of every four eggs put in the hatcher at Cornell produce live chicks. This is an excellent record and equals the success at hatcheries in the poultry industry.

It is a time of furious activity for both birds and humans around Peregrine Palace. The workers usually feed the chicks for the first week or so.

"For some strange reason," a biologist at Cornell says, "many captive falcons and other birds of prey are likely to eat their young at the time of hatching or in the first few days out of the shell. But the same birds that will eat newly hatched chicks usually will take care of older young."

The young men and women who work with Tom Cade generally keep the chicks in the hatcher for a day. When the chicks dry, the handlers fluff out their down with a very soft brush. They must also be certain that the hatchery remains clean so that the chicks do not pick up diseases or infections.

Then they move the chicks to styrofoam chests in which they can control the amount of heat. If the chicks huddle together but do not call repeatedly or look uncomfortable, the workers know the temperature is just right.

The chick is fed as soon as it is strong enough to lift its head and open its mouth. The workers may start feeding a chick by sticking a tiny sliver of meat into its throat with a pair of forceps. The forceps have blunt tips and will not cut the chick's skin. The chick is fed mostly ground quail.

The handlers must feed the chicks in small amounts every two to four hours. As the number of chicks increases, feeding them becomes quite a job. The handlers are able to feed many chicks quickly by filling a plastic bag with ground meat. Then they go from chick to chick, squeezing a portion into each tiny mouth, just as you would decorate the top of a cake.

After a week or two the chicks are given to the adult peregrines. They carry on the job of feeding much as they do in the wild. One pair of adults at Cornell took care of four chicks and, as soon as they were removed, took care of another five.

The young birds are left in the care of adults for several weeks. During that time they become imprinted—they learn to recognize their parents as peregrine falcons and therefore they will respond to other peregrines in the future. At that point they are taken from the parents, either to be paired in chambers of their own or made ready to be released into the wild.

In 1973 there were three pairs of adult peregrines that mated successfully at Peregrine Palace. One pair, Heinz Meng's Peale's peregrines, laid nine eggs in two clutches, from which seven young were hatched. In all, twenty-one peregrines were raised at Peregrine Palace that year.

Nothing like this had ever been done with peregrines before. Tom Cade and his helpers knew then that they could rear large numbers of birds for their project to restore the wild population. They reared twenty-three young in 1974 and twenty-four in 1975. By 1976 the project also had "peregrine palaces" in operation in Pennsylvania and Colorado. These three laboratories produced a total of sixty-nine young peregrines. The most exciting news was that some of the young hatched at Cornell in 1973 began to produce young of their own.

"Pretty soon we will be turning out between two hundred and two hundred and fifty young peregrines a year," Tom Cade said. "That will be more young than peregrines ever raised in the wild in the eastern United States."

The next step was to put young peregrines into the wild—and keep them there.

11
HACKING

It is time to return to those four young peregrines who were being put into their new home on top of the test tower at Carroll Island. They are now about six weeks old. With food and exercise in the big plywood box they have become large and strong.

But their handlers cannot simply remove the bars covering the opening to the box and let the peregrines fly off to freedom. The birds still don't have the experience to live in the wild. Hatched in captivity at Cornell and reared in the box on the tower, they still know nothing about hunting for food or defending themselves against predators. They still must learn to be wild.

At this point the knowledge and skill of the falconers once more becomes important. Tom Cade and his helpers selected one of the oldest methods of training falcons for sport and used it to train their falcons for freedom. It is called hacking.

Falconers used to collect many of their hunting birds from eyries while they were still chicks. They raised them by hand at home. When the birds were ready to fly, they were still not any good for hunting because it takes experience to be able to catch healthy wild birds and mammals.

The falconer set up what he called a hacking station. This was a box much like the one at Carroll Island, fastened to a pole or high tree stump. He tethered—or tied—his young falcon in the box and fed it by raising food on a stick so that it could not see him. The falconer knew that to develop his bird's wildness and its ability to hunt it should have as little contact as possible with human beings.

When the falcon was ready to fly, the falconer untied it. The bird was free to fly out over the surrounding countryside, where, by instinct, it began chasing other birds. At first it wasn't very skillful at hunting and seldom caught anything. But the young falcon knew there

---

Biologists use a man-made tower to release captive-bred peregrines into the wild. The hacking box sits on top of the tower.

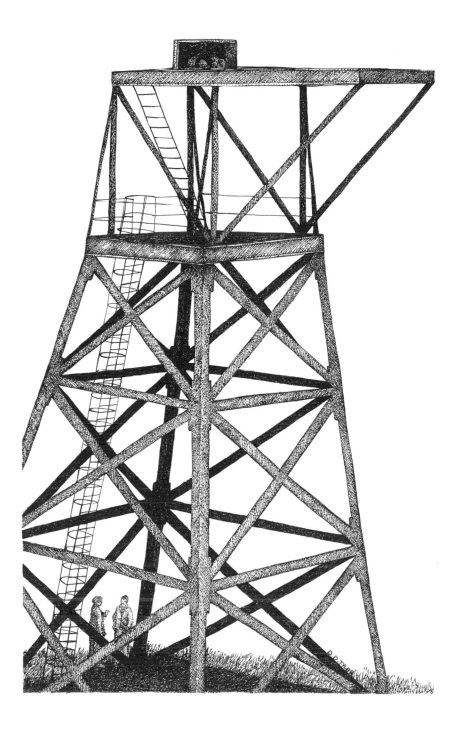

was always food at the hacking box and returned there whenever it grew really hungry.

By this method the young falcon remained well fed until it learned the skills of hunting in the wild. When the falconer saw that his bird was catching most of his own food, he trapped it and used it as a hunting bird in the sport of falconry.

The young peregrines at Carroll Island were taught to be wild through hacking. The bars had kept them safe for a while. There was no chance of them falling to their death as they might have while exercising or squabbling over food at a wild eyrie. The bars also took the place of parents, which protect the young in the wild against owls and other predators.

One day the handlers removed the bars from the hacking box. Three of the young peregrines flew out at once. They flew well, circling the island and coming back to perch on the box. The fourth peregrine—a female—did not fly at once. She waited a day because she was larger and heavier than the others and needed more confidence to take off from the hacking box.

Dr. F. Prescott Ward, a veterinarian who was studying Carroll Island's wildlife for the army, kept a close watch on the young peregrines. He watched from a distance during the first few days as they learned to fly. It was a thrilling sight. After a few days the peregrines began to chase starlings, red-winged blackbirds, and shore birds. Once three of the young peregrines chased a large turkey vulture high into the sky above the island. Although they often caught up with the other birds, the peregrines were not skillful at using their feet to make the kill, and the prey always escaped.

Dr. Ward had a supply of wild pigeons that he used for training the peregrines. He climbed the tower and tossed one of the pigeons into the air. To handicap the pigeon he had plucked some of its flight feathers or taped its eyes shut. The peregrines learned to follow the fluttering pigeon and strike it cleanly from the air with their talons. They were getting a taste for killing other birds.

For several more days Dr. Ward left food in the hacking box. Then, after a day on which he had not fed the peregrines, he arrived at the tower to see one of the falcons feeding on something. A soft wind carried the prey's dark feathers, tinged with green and white, away from the tower. After the falcon finished eating and flew off, Dr. Ward examined the prey's feathers. The falcon had killed and eaten a green heron. She was a hunter at last.

Tom Cade came to the island from Cornell to see how the peregrines were doing. Dr. Ward tossed a pigeon into the air. It flew in circles for a moment and one of the peregrines flew after it. The pigeon turned and headed for the trees in the distance, the peregrine close behind.

"A tail chase!" Cade called to the others with him.

For a moment it was an exciting chase. The pigeon flew for its life toward the trees. David Zimmerman, a writer who was with Cade, described the scene as the pigeon put on a burst of speed:

"This seemed to provoke the peregrine, which climbed swiftly above it. They were at the trees. The peregrine stooped half-heartedly. Missed. Veered. Broke off the pursuit. Wheeled and flopped back to the gun tower. And resumed its sunbath. The pigeon flew away."

Dr. Ward turned to Cade and grinned. "They don't want this handout, Tom. They're catching blue jays and blackbirds and all those other things. When they catch prey once . . . that's all. They're self-sufficient."

Before giving the peregrines their full freedom, the biologists captured them once more. They cemented a tiny radio, weighing only a quarter of an ounce, to a long tail feather on each bird. The radio would send signals for a few weeks and allow the biologists to keep track of them. When the bird molted its tail feather, the radio would fall off too.

The biologists also attached blue bands to the peregrines' legs. The bands were printed with large white numbers and letters that could be read at a distance by biologists using high-powered spotting scopes. In this way, if the peregrines are seen somewhere in the future, the biologists may be able to tell where they were released.

These peregrines were not the only ones hatched at Cornell that were entering the wild. Cade and his helpers selected other good sites for hacking young peregrines in the East.

Sometimes the hacking boxes were put on man-made towers, as they were at Carroll Island and at the headquarters of the Massachusetts Audubon Society in Lincoln, Massachusetts. At other places the boxes were put on ledges where wild peregrines had once nested. Heinz Meng helped to set up a hacking box on the same ledge where peregrines had an eyrie high above the Hudson River valley during the 1930s. A biologist who had visited that eyrie nearly forty years before watched the young peregrines as they were released from the hacking box. "These young falcons certainly act as though they know they belong to this cliff," he said happily.

Many dedicated people worked very hard to make the release program a success. Young men and women served without pay for weeks at a time, working sometimes twenty-four hours a day, to guard the eyries and feed the young until they were able to take care of themselves. These people wanted only to see peregrines in the wild again.

The falconers and scientists got more help from the

Downy tufts still show through the growing feathers of a young peregrine when it is in the hacking box.

birds themselves in the West. Although the population of peregrines was in trouble in the Rocky Mountains, there were still some pairs raising young at wild eyries.

James H. Enderson, a biologist and falconer at Colorado College, closely watched a wild pair of peregrines at their eyrie in a Colorado mountain gorge. The falcon laid a clutch of eggs, but it was the same old story. The eggs broke or did not hatch. When the falcon laid a second clutch, they were infertile too.

Working quickly before the adults abandoned the eyrie, Enderson replaced the infertile eggs with two eggs he had taken from prairie falcons—a more numerous species in the West. The peregrines incubated these strange eggs and one of them hatched.

Meanwhile, Enderson had two peregrine chicks sent to him by plane from Cornell. He removed the prairie falcon chick and put the two peregrine chicks in the eyrie. The adults raised them as if they were their own, caring for them until they were able to hunt for themselves.

In the Rocky Mountains, as well as in eastern states, captive-bred young peregrines were going into the wild. How were they making out?

12
FACING THE WILD

At the end of July a friend told Dr. Ward that there was a photograph of one of "his" peregrines in a Baltimore newspaper. Ward couldn't believe it at first. But when he saw a copy of the newspaper, there was a peregrine all right, with a band on its leg, perched on the ledge of an office building in Baltimore.

Ward made some phone calls. He learned that a lawyer had seen the bird on a ledge outside the window of the law firm's library, thirty-two stories high. The lawyer knew it was a hawk, but he had no idea what kind. Luckily there was an encyclopedia at hand in the library,

City dwellers are startled to see a full-grown peregrine perched on the ledge of a skyscraper.

and thumbing through it hurriedly, the lawyer found a picture of a peregrine falcon. The markings matched those of the bird on the ledge. He called a newspaper editor and the peregrine got its picture in the paper.

Ward asked the lawyer about the band on the bird's leg. The lawyer said it was light blue, like those worn by the young peregrines released at Carroll Island, twenty miles away. The batteries in the tiny radio carried by all four young peregrines had failed after a few days and Ward had no idea where the birds had gone. Now he knew about one of them—it was living in downtown Baltimore, eating city pigeons.

Later in the summer other reports came in. One of the peregrines was seen at the Chesapeake Bay Bridge, forty miles south of Carroll Island, chasing shore birds. Two other peregrines were killing pigeons around the grain elevators in Baltimore Harbor.

Tom Cade and his helpers, after studying the reports, thought it likely that these were the birds released at Carroll Island. All four were making a living in the wild —if the vicinity of Baltimore can be called "wild." The Carroll Island peregrines were following the same pattern as those that used to nest on the Hudson River cliffs— entering a city to feed on pigeons.

Some of the other peregrines released in the East were not so lucky. Two of the three young given their freedom on the grounds of the Massachusetts Audubon Society seemed to have succeeded, but the radio fixed to the third peregrine stopped sending signals shortly after the release. No one knows exactly what happened to the bird, but Cade believes that it tangled with a large electric power transformer and was electrocuted.

Three other young birds were released near Cornell in a gorge where peregrines once had a wild eyrie. When one of the birds disappeared, Cornell biologists tracked it down by its radio signals and found it had been killed and its head eaten off. A few days later they found the remains of a second young peregrine that had been killed and partly eaten. The biologists had seen great horned owls near the gorge. These large predators will kill young peregrines and other hawks if they can catch them. Biologists estimated that the cost of raising the two young peregrines had been nearly $6,000. The horned owls, then, had eaten a very expensive supper.

"Horned owls won't catch young peregrines at wild eyries as a rule because the parents will chase the owls away," Tom Cade said. "We recaptured the third young peregrine at the hacking box right away and brought it back to Peregrine Palace. When we release young birds in the future, we will trap the great horned owls living close by and transport them to some other area."

These setbacks saddened the workers on the Peregrine

Project of course, but they knew that all creatures in the wild face such risks from predators and accidents. It was harder to accept the actions taken against the young peregrines by some human beings.

In 1974 Heinz Meng had released two of his captive-bred peregrines from a tower on the campus at New Paltz. The peregrines remained in the area, occasionally chasing small birds. After a few days Meng received a telephone call from a man who refused to identify himself: "Can't you do something about those killer birds on campus?" the man asked.

A few days later the peregrines were missing. Meng searched for them in the surrounding countryside. All he ever found was a wing of his female peregrine, lying in a wooded area near the campus. "The wing could have been cut off by a sharp knife or a hatchet," Meng said. It was his guess that someone had shot the birds and cut them up.

The next year Tom Cade and his assistant, Jim Weaver, planned to release some peregrines at an old eyrie near Deerfield, Massachusetts. Some residents of

---

The great horned owl, which is named for the tuft of feathers on each side of its head, is a fierce predator that will kill young peregrines if it gets the chance.

the area, however, protested this plan. They were afraid that the peregrines would eat all the songbirds. The local newspaper also published an editorial against the plan.

Cade and Weaver decided not to release the birds there. They knew that the fears about the songbirds were silly, because only a very few peregrines can live in one area and they capture only a small fraction of the local birds. Although most of the people around Deerfield seemed to want to have the young peregrines, Cade and Weaver remembered what had happened to Heinz Meng's birds. They decided instead to release their peregrines in a protected marsh along the New Jersey coast.

Then in 1975, the Cornell biologists released sixteen young peregrines in the East. Three of them, as we have seen, were killed and one was recaptured and brought back to Peregrine Palace. The other twelve birds learned to hunt and care for themselves in the wild. More and more young peregrines are being released each year. In spite of the few setbacks, peregrine falcons are flying once more in the eastern United States.

In the summer of 1976 a young falcon perched on the cliffs above the lower Hudson River where she had an excellent view of the tall ships that sailed past New York City to celebrate the nation's Bicentennial. And in western Massachusetts Joseph A. Hagar, now eighty-one years old, watched a young peregrine fly across the face of a cliff where he had studied a wild eyrie for the last time more than a quarter of a century before.

"We've got them in the air," Tom Cade said. "The big test is whether our birds will occupy their own eyries and begin to raise their own young."

13
A NEW POPULATION

No one believes the struggle to bring back the peregrine falcon is won. There are still too many dangers. Although the use of DDT and other long-lasting pesticides has been stopped in many countries of Europe and North America, those poisons are still in the environment. Other countries, especially in Central and South America, still use large amounts of the harmful chemicals. Peregrines that migrate to those southern regions will pick up the poisons.

But the way is prepared for the peregrine's return to the eastern United States. It will not be the same population that lived there once. That was wiped out. If the birds begin to breed there again, it will be a new population, created from captive Peale's peregrines and birds from the far north.

The United States government has put the peregrine

98

falcon on the endangered species list. That means the peregrine will receive special protection. The government pays a reward for help in convicting people who kill those birds or take their eggs and young. A New Jersey man, who shot one of the young falcons in 1975, had it stuffed and mounted in his home—complete with its identification band and radio transmitter! Federal agents took him to court in 1977. The man agreed to pay $2,000 to Cornell's Peregrine Fund.

The federal government has also formed "peregrine recovery teams" to help bring back the bird to parts of the country where it is endangered. The National Audubon Society is contributing money and manpower to this effort.

In the summer of 1976 Stan Temple of the Peregrine Project visited a tower at Barnegat Bay on the New Jersey coast, where young peregrines had been released before. He brought with him several peregrine chicks from Cornell that he planned to put in the hacking box in the tower. But when he looked in the box he found he had been beaten to it. A pair of barn owls had taken over the box and were raising their own young inside.

Temple found another nest for the barn owls. Then he put the young peregrines in the hacking box. The next day, just as dusk came on, a young tercel flew along the shore and landed on the tower next to the box. He wore a blue band on one leg, and by his plumage Temple knew that he was a year old. He was one of the birds released from that hacking box the year before.

Each night from then on the tercel flew to the tower to spend the night. The two adult barn owls, whose nest had been moved near by, sometimes joined him for the night. These owls, which feed mostly on mice and other small rodents, would not bother the young peregrines once they were released from the box.

When the young peregrines began to fly, the tercel joined them, following them almost like an older brother. He chased them through the air and dove at them playfully. When they returned to the tower for food he joined them and found an easy meal.

"There is no doubt that this tercel has taken the Barnegat Tower as his chosen eyrie," Tom Cade said. "All he needs to do to complete the cycle is to attract a female to his nest."

The peregrine falcon faces an uncertain future in the modern world.

ACKNOWLEDGMENTS

The authors want to thank Tom J. Cade of the Cornell University Laboratory of Ornithology and Richard L. Plunkett of the National Audubon Society for their help during the preparation of this book.

Joseph A. Hagar's descriptions of peregrine falcons in Chapters 4 and 5 may be found in more complete form in Bent's *Life Histories of North American Birds of Prey*, which is included in the list of books below. Parts of Chapter 11 are based on David R. Zimmerman's article "That the Peregrine Shall Live" in *Audubon*, November 1975. Parts of several other chapters are based on various issues of the Peregrine Fund's *Newsletter*.

The authors found the following books especially helpful during their research:

J. A. Baker. *The Peregrine*. New York: Harper & Row, 1967.

Acknowledgments

Arthur Cleveland Bent. *Life Histories of North American Birds of Prey.* 2 vols. Washington, D.C.: Smithsonian Institution, 1937–38.

Leslie Brown and Dean Amadon. *Eagles, Hawks and Falcons of the World.* 2 vols. New York: McGraw-Hill, 1968.

Joseph J. Hickey, ed. *Peregrine Falcon Populations: Their Biology and Decline.* Madison: University of Wisconsin Press, 1969.

John Kaufmann and Heinz Meng. *Falcons Return: Restoring an Endangered Species.* New York: William Morrow, 1975.

Alice Schick. *The Peregrine Falcons.* Pictures by Peter Parnall. New York: The Dial Press, 1975.

—ADA AND FRANK GRAHAM

104

INDEX

105

Index

Index

Index

32–39, 66, 67, 71, 76; misconceptions about, 17–18, 31; naming of, 10, 67–69; nesting habits of, 25, 31, 39, 49–51 (*see also* eyrie); nest robbers and, 2, 28–31; playfulness of, 100; plumage of, 11, 44, 45, 88; poisoning of, 2, 48, 59–64, 89; preening of, 38–39; protection of, 24–25, 98–99; range of, 10, 49; release program, *see* Peregrine Project; senses of, 12–13; sex differentiation in, 34–35, 75–76; shooting of, 2; size of, 34–35; speed of, 11–12, 28; subspecies of, 67–69, 70–71 (map), 98; trapping of, 2; "world's most successful bird," 1, 10, 49; young eaten by, 78. *See also* birds of prey; falcon; hawk

Peregrine Fund, 73, 99
Peregrine Palace, 74, 76, 79–80, 93, 96
Peregrine Project, 1–4, 65–66, 72, 73–100
peregrine recovery teams, 99
pesticides: long–range effect of, 59–64

pheasant, 17
Philip of England, 71
pigeon, 3, 37–38, 50, 51, 53, 54, 57, 85–86, 92
pigeon handlers, 51
plover, 11
poison: chain effect of, 60, 61–64; long-range effects of, 98; peregrine destruction by, 2, 48, 59–64, 89
pole traps, 18, 19, 20
Potomac River, eyries on, 31
prairie falcon, 61, 89
predator: definition of, 5–6
predators: hatred of, 16; misconceptions about, 17–20; protection of, 17, 22–25, 98–99

Quabbin Reservoir, Massachusetts, 55
quail, 3, 8, 76, 79
Queen Charlotte Islands, 69

rabbit, 8, 16, 76
raccoon, 55
radio: use of, for bird tracking, 86, 92, 93, 99
rat, 16, 76
Ratcliffe, Derek A., 57–59

110

Index

Index

Walden Pond, 17
Ward, Dr. F. Prescott, 84–86,
  90–92
waterfowl, 18
Weaver, Jim, 95–96
West Virginia: eyries in, 31

Wildlife protection, 18, 22–
  23, 52, 65–66, 96
woodpecker, 21
worm, 5, 61

Zimmerman, David, 86